WOMEN'S SOCCER SCRAPBOOK

THE ULTIMATE INSIDER'S GUIDE

FOREWORD BY KRISTINE LILLY, U.S. NATIONAL TEAM MEMBER

BY JILL POTVIN SCHOFF

SOMERVILLE HOUSE, USA
NEW YORK

Grateful acknowledgment to SOCCER JR.
for permission to use some material from
the following articles written by Jill Potvin Schoff:
  "Looking Back," January/February 1999
  "Two Thumbs Up" and "Coming Up Roses,"
   September/October 1999
  "Great Expectations," May/June 1999.

With special thanks to Phil Stephens for the use
of his photographs.
Cover photographs: main, Elsa/Allsport; left and
middle, JBW/International Sports Images; far right,
David Cannon/Allsport. Back cover and dedication
photographs: Tony Duffy/Allsport.

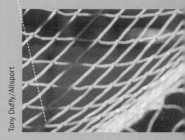

Tony Duffy/Allsport

ISBN: 1-58184-089-6   A B C D E F G H I J

Printed in China
Designer: Carol Moskot

Somerville House, USA is distributed by
Penguin Putnam Books for Young Readers,
345 Hudson Street, NY, NY 10014

Published in Canada by
Somerville House Publishing
a division of Somerville House Books Limited
3080 Yonge Street, Suite 5000
Toronto, ON
M4N 3N1

e-mail: sombooks@goodmedia.com
Website: www.sombooks.com

To my parents, grandparents, and husband, Eric.

You make me believe that anything is possible.

— J.P.S.

CONTENTS

INTRODUCTION

England's Dick Kerr Ladies were pioneers of women's soccer in the 1920s.

EXCITING. AMAZING. INSPIRING.
This is the world of women's soccer today. In 1999, for the first time in history, a women's team sporting event captured the attention of the world. More than 658,000 fans attended the 1999 Women's World Cup games, and more than a billion people worldwide watched them on television! When the U.S. Women's National Team players stood on the field, smiling and crying as they accepted their trophy, people all over the world smiled and cried right along with them. Players like Mia Hamm, Brandi Chastain, and Briana Scurry became heroes and inspired people to look at soccer—and women's sports—in a new light.

The Early Years

Women didn't always get so much attention. In fact, women haven't always played soccer. Soccer started as a "man's game," and was considered too wild and dangerous for women. There is some evidence that women played in France in the 12th century and in Scotland in the 1700s. But, for the most part, women didn't play until the rules for soccer, as we know it today, were written in 1863 in England. These new rules made soccer less violent, and more women began to play. During World War I, women started to work in factories because the men were off fighting in the war. As women gained a place in the workforce, they also gained a place on the soccer field.

The most famous of the early women's teams was England's Dick Kerr Ladies Team. In 1920 the Dick Kerr Ladies were hugely popular and played in front of crowds of up to 53,000 people! But the English Football Association (which owned most of the soccer stadiums) banned women from using their fields, thus slowing down the development of the women's game in England. Still, women's soccer continued to grow in Europe and America.

federally funded educational institutions to provide equal opportunity for women in sports), and high schools and colleges around the country started developing girls' sports teams. This encouraged more and more girls to become athletes. Soccer really caught on because it was seen as an alternate fall sport to football.

By 1985, the United States had formed a women's national team. In 1991 the U.S. Women's National Team joined 12 other countries in China at the first "official" Federation Internationale de Football Association (FIFA) Women's World Championship. The United States returned home with the trophy,

> Female soccer players in the United States have all kinds of opportunities: they can play soccer in high school, watch their favorite soccer stars on television, get a college soccer scholarship, and even represent their country in the Olympics.

At first women just played for schools and clubs. There were no professional leagues for them to play in and there were no national teams to join. In soccer, the most important games are played between teams that represent their countries. Each nation gathers its best players and forms a "national team." These teams play each other often and take part in international tournaments.

Women's Soccer Takes Off

The formation of women's national teams in the 1970s was an important step in the development of the sport. The first unofficial women's world championship took place in 1970; Denmark defeated Italy to win the tournament.

Another important development was the start of girls' youth soccer teams. The United States passed the "Title IX" amendment in 1972 (which required

but most newspapers and TV stations didn't even mention it. Women's soccer still had a way to go.

Soccer Today

My, how things have changed. Female soccer players in the United States have all kinds of opportunities: they can play soccer in high school, watch their favorite soccer stars on television, get a college soccer scholarship, and even represent their country in the Olympics. As the 21st century begins, interest in women's soccer all over the globe is at an all-time high. In places as diverse as Iran and the island of Samoa, women are falling in love with the game.

As women's soccer grows, it is attracting more and more fans. These fans, like you, can't wait for the 2000 Olympics to begin. The following chapters will tell you everything you need to know about the teams and stars who will be there!

DID YOU KNOW? The British call soccer "football," Brazilians call it "futbol," and Italians call it "calcio."

Not long ago, girls weren't allowed to play soccer. Now millions play all over the world.

Phil Stephens Photography

CHAPTER 1

THE STARS AND STRIPES FLY HIGH

The 1991 Women's World Cup

The first Women's World Cup took place in China from November 16 to 30, 1991. Back then it wasn't even called a "World Cup"—it was called the "Women's World Championship" instead. The women didn't care what it was called, though. They just wanted to find out which country had the best women's soccer team in the world. The only way to find out was to have a tournament just like the men did. (The men's World Cup is much older. The first one took place in 1930.)

Finally, in November 1991, twelve women's national teams got the chance to show their stuff: Brazil, China, Chinese Taipei (now called Taiwan), Denmark, Germany, Italy, Japan, New Zealand, Nigeria, Norway, Sweden, and the United States. The tournament didn't get much attention. In fact,

12

The Final

The championship game would be between Norway and the United States. Norway focused on defense, trying to stop the speed of the American attack. In the 20th minute, 19-year-old Mia Hamm was tripped and an indirect free kick was called. Shannon Higgins took the kick and placed it perfectly for Michelle Akers-Stahl to head into the net for the first American goal. But a determined Norway—led by star striker Linda Medalen—evened the score eight minutes later.

Midway through the second half, the score was still 1–1, and neither side was able to gain an advantage. The tension was rising because both teams knew that the next goal would likely decide the game. Suddenly, a Norwegian defender tried to backpass the ball to her keeper, but Akers-Stahl intercepted. She flew past the goalie and placed the ball perfectly in the net! A few minutes later the final whistle blew, and the United States won the first Women's World Championship.

DID YOU KNOW?
Six U.S. players have played in all three Women's World Cups: Michelle Akers, Joy Fawcett, Julie Foudy, Mia Hamm, Kristine Lilly, and Carla Overbeck.

WOMEN'S WORLD CHAMPIONSHIP
FINAL STANDINGS

The First Round

Two points were awarded for a win, one point for a tie, and zero points for a loss.
(W = Wins   L = Losses   T = Ties   GF = Goals For   GA = Goals Against   PTS = Points)

Group A

TEAM	W	L	T	GF	GA	PTS
China	2	0	1	10	3	5
Norway	2	1	0	6	5	4
Denmark	1	1	1	6	4	3
New Zealand	0	3	0	1	11	0

China 4, Norway 0   Denmark 3, New Zealand 0   Norway 4, New Zealand 0
China 2, Denmark 2   China 4, New Zealand 1   Norway 2, Denmark 1

Group B

TEAM	W	L	T	GF	GA	PTS
U.S.	3	0	0	11	2	6
Sweden	2	1	0	12	3	4
Brazil	1	2	0	1	7	2
Japan	0	3	0	0	12	0

Brazil 1, Japan 0   U.S. 3, Sweden 2   Sweden 8, Japan 0   U.S. 5, Brazil 0
U.S. 3, Japan 0   Sweden 2, Brazil 0

Group C

TEAM	W	L	T	GF	GA	PTS
Germany	3	0	0	9	0	6
Italy	2	1	0	6	2	4
Chinese Taipei	1	2	0	2	8	2
Nigeria	0	3	0	0	7	0

Germany 4, Nigeria 0   Italy 5, Chinese Taipei 0   Italy 1, Nigeria 0
Germany 3, Chinese Taipei 0   Chinese Taipei 2, Nigeria 0   Germany 2, Italy 0

The Quarterfinals

Germany 2, Denmark 1 (OT)	Sweden 1, China 0
Norway 3, Italy 2 (OT)	U.S. 7, Chinese Taipei 0

The Semifinals

Norway 4, Sweden 1	U.S. 5, Germany 2

The Third-place Game

Germany 4, Sweden 0

The Final

U.S. 2, Norway 1

Norway's keeper, Bente Nordby *(center)*, raises the Women's World Cup trophy with some of her teammates.

NORWAY 2
TAKES OVER THE
WORLD

The 1995 Women's World Cup

Chris Cole/Allsport

The second World Cup was held in Sweden from June 5 to 18, 1995. The United States was there to defend their title, but they knew it would not be easy. China wanted to redeem themselves, Norway had a grudge to settle, Germany was especially strong, and the home team would have the support of the crowd.

Germany, Sweden, Japan, and Brazil were in Group A. They were joined by Norway, England, Canada, and Nigeria in Group B. The nations in Group C were the United States, China, Denmark, and Australia.

The First Round

The U.S. team struggled against China in its first game and had to settle for a 3–3 tie. Michelle Akers, the team's leading goal scorer, sustained a concussion and a sprained knee just seven minutes into the match. She had to sit out the next three games. Despite the loss of Akers, the U.S. team won its next two games and first place in Group C over China.

Sweden suffered a shocking 1–0 loss to Brazil in its opening game, but the home team recovered and later rallied to beat Germany 3–2. Germany still finished ahead of Sweden in their group. Norway had no trouble in Group B, scoring 17 goals and allowing none in the first round. England finished second behind the Norwegians.

The Quarterfinals

China got some revenge for their 1991 Women's World Championship loss in the quarterfinals,

when it beat Sweden. Germany, Norway, and the U.S. all won their games pretty easily.

The Semifinals

Germany was evenly matched with China in their semifinal game. The Germans finally scored on a goal by Bettina Wiegmann in the second half, and China couldn't equalize. The game ended 1–0.

Against Norway in the semifinals, Akers played a full game for the United States, despite not being fully recovered from her injuries. Without a completely healthy Akers leading the attack, the U.S. team lost 1–0. It was their first World Cup defeat. The U.S. women vowed that they

DID YOU KNOW? Mia Hamm played goalie at the end of a game in the 1995 Women's World Cup when Briana Scurry was ejected. No more substitutes were allowed, so a field player had to fill in! Mia held the other team scoreless, making one save.

Mia Hamm (No. 9) was shut down by the Norwegian defense in the semifinals.

would win back their title, and they set their sights on the 1996 Olympics in Atlanta with fierce determination.

The Third-place Game

The U.S. team still had to face China to decide who would finish in third place. The United States took the lead halfway through the first half with a header by Tisha Venturini. Goalkeeper Briana Scurry had a great game and kept the Chinese attack shut down. Mia Hamm put the U.S. team ahead 2–0, and that's the way the game ended. The United States wouldn't go home with the trophy, but at least they got the bronze.

The Final

Norway faced Germany in the championship game. The Norwegians dominated most of the first half. Hege Riise scored the first goal for Norway with a blast from about 18 yards out. Minutes later, Norway scored again, when Marianne Pettersen captured a loose ball in the penalty box and kicked it past the German keeper. The Germans took over during the second half, but they couldn't score. The game ended 2–0, and Norway lifted the trophy in triumph.

WOMEN'S WORLD CUP
FINAL STANDINGS

The First Round

Three points were awarded for a win, one point for a tie, and zero points for a loss.

Group A

TEAM	W	L	T	GF	GA	PTS
Germany	2	1	0	9	4	6
Sweden	2	1	0	5	3	6
Japan	1	2	0	2	4	3
Brazil	1	2	0	3	8	3

Germany 1, Japan 0   Brazil 1, Sweden 0   Sweden 3, Germany 2
Japan 2, Brazil 1   Sweden 2, Japan 0   Germany 6, Brazil 1

Group B

TEAM	W	L	T	GF	GA	PTS
Norway	3	0	0	17	0	9
England	2	1	0	6	6	6
Canada	0	2	1	5	13	1
Nigeria	0	2	1	5	14	1

Norway 8, Nigeria 0   England 3, Canada 2   Norway 2, England 0
Nigeria 3, Canada 3   Norway 7, Canada 0   England 3, Nigeria 2

Group C

TEAM	W	L	T	GF	GA	PTS
U.S.	2	0	1	9	4	7
China	2	0	1	10	6	7
Denmark	1	2	0	6	5	3
Australia	0	3	0	3	13	0

U.S. 3, China 3   Denmark 5, Australia 0   U.S. 2, Denmark 0
China 4, Australia 2   U.S. 4, Australia 1   China 3, Denmark 1

The Quarterfinals

U.S. 4, Japan 0   Norway 3, Denmark 1

Germany 3, England 0   China 1, Sweden 1*

The Semifinals

Norway 1, U.S. 0   Germany 1, China 0

The Third-place Game

U.S. 2, China 0

The Final

Norway 2, Germany 0

* (China wins 4-3 on penalty kicks.)

3

THE FIRST OLYMPIC CHAMPIONS

The 1996 Olympics

At the 1996 Atlanta Games, women's soccer was an Olympic event for the first time. From July 21 to August 1, eight teams competed for soccer supremacy and a gold medal. China, the U.S., Sweden, and Denmark were in Group E. The teams in Group F were Norway, Brazil, Germany, and Japan.

Nobody knew who would walk away with the gold medal. Would it be Norway, which had just won the Women's World Cup the year before? Or the United States, which had vowed to settle for no less than first place? Or would China or Germany end up on top? Tension was high as the first game kicked off on July 21.

The Americans Aim High

America's first opponent was Denmark. A record crowd gathered to watch the game at the Citrus

David Cannon/Allsport

The U.S. women jump for joy after Brandi Chastain's penalty kick.

Ghana's Elizabeth Baidu *(No. 5)* and
Australia's Cheryl Salisbury play tough.

Nigerians. She turned 16 on May 17, 1999.

June 23

This was a day for blowouts. Defending champion Norway steam-rolled Canada 7–1. World Cup newcomer Russia displayed surprising promise in its 5–0 thrashing of Japan. China showed off its strength in a 7–0 win over Ghana, with star striker Sun Wen scoring a hat trick.

June 24

During the first match of the day, Brazil took an early lead over Italy on a goal by Sissi. Italy had the chance to equalize on a penalty

why it was considered one of the real threats of the tournament. The Brazilians played without injured striker Roseli, but Pretinha and Sissi picked up the slack—and then some. Both scored hat tricks against a weak Mexican team. The game ended 7–1.

June 20: AUSTRALIA vs. GHANA

Australia and Ghana played one of the most physical games of the tournament. The teams racked up six yellow cards, and Ghana's Barikisu Tettey-Quao was the first player in the tournament to receive a red card. The red card forced Ghana to play a person short for the rest of the match, but the team still managed to pull off a tie, due largely to talented young goalkeeper Memunatu Sulemana.

A tie was considered a success for newcomer Ghana, but not for Germany, which had to settle for a 1–1 draw with Italy. Germany was the only top-seeded team that didn't win its first game.

June 20

Nigeria's 2–1 win over North Korea was its first win in Women's World Cup history. The Nigerians had five losses and one tie in the last two tournaments. The youngest player in the tournament, Ifeanyichukwu Chiejene, started in midfield for the

kick, but captain Antonella Carta's shot was blocked. The Brazilians won 2–0 and secured a place in the quarterfinals.

The U.S.–Nigeria game began with a shocking Nigerian goal in the second minute. The U.S.

women calmed down and tied the score in the 19th minute, when veteran center midfielder Michelle Akers helped force a Nigerian own goal. Akers charged toward the Nigerian goal. While attempting to prevent Akers from scoring, a Nigerian defender knocked the ball into her own net by mistake. Hamm scored a minute later and started an all-out scoring spree that didn't end till the American team had tallied six goals in the half. The game ended 7–1.

Denmark suffered a surprising 3–1 loss to World Cup newcomer North Korea and, to make matters worse, lost forward Marlene Kristensen, when she slipped and broke her leg early in the game. The previous day another Danish forward, Karina Christensen, had broken her nose while practicing. The unlucky Danes ended up leaving the tournament without a win.

In the last game of the evening, Inka Grings's hat trick helped Germany beat Mexico 6–0. Mexico ended up placing last in the tournament, having been outscored 15–1 in three games.

June 26

China won its next game 3–1, securing first place in its group and sending Australia home. Ghana and Sweden fought fiercely for the right to advance with China. The young Swedish team won 2–0 but lost striker Hanna Ljungberg to a knee injury. Ghana was sent packing, but the team showed promise.

In the last game of the day, Norway had no trouble beating Japan 4–0 and securing first place in its group.

June 27

One of the best games of the tournament was Brazil versus Germany. Birgit Prinz scored first for Germany, but Brazil scored two in a row. Germany tied

the game with a penalty kick and then pulled ahead with a goal by Steffi Jones. It looked like Germany was going to win, but in the fourth minute of injury time—seconds before the ref blew the whistle—Maicon scored the tying goal for Brazil. The tie was a big deal because it meant Brazil finished first in the group, leaving Germany to play the United States in the quarterfinals.

The U.S. had virtually assured itself a quarterfinal berth (North Korea would have to beat the U.S. team 13–0 to prevent it from advancing!), so the team rested some of its starters. Shannon MacMillan and Tisha Venturini got their first starts of the tournament. They confirmed their team's faith by doing all of the scoring. MacMillan blasted one home from the top of the box and Venturini scored not one but two diving headers. It's hard to say which was more impressive—Venturini's headers or the cool cartwheel back-flip she did in celebration! With the win,

JBW/International Sports Images

Germany couldn't stop Brazil's Maicon (No. 7).

the Americans placed first in their group, and Nigeria came in second.

The Quarterfinals

June 30

The United States, Brazil, Norway, China, Nigeria, Germany, Russia, and Sweden all advanced to the quarterfinals. The stakes were now higher—a loss meant a team was out of the tournament. No ties were allowed; if necessary, overtime and penalty kicks would decide a game.

In the first quarterfinal match, Russia faced Olympic silver medalist China. The Russians fought hard and defended beautifully, but they couldn't stop the Chinese attack. Eighteen-year-old Pu Wei, the youngest Chinese player, scored right before halftime. Jin Yan scored in the second half to give China a 2–0 victory.

In the next game, Norway defeated Sweden with three goals in the second half, including one by star striker Marianne Pettersen. It looked like Sweden was going to lose 3–0 until Malin Mostrom scored in the 91st minute. Despite the loss, Sweden played well, and many believe it will be a team to watch at the Women's World Cup in 2003.

July 1

In a shocking start to the U.S.–Germany quarterfinal game, a miscommunication between Brandi

Chastain and goaltender Briana Scurry led to a heartbreaking own goal for the United States. Tiffeny Milbrett tied the score, but Germany pulled ahead again right before halftime. Chastain redeemed herself in the second half, when she redirected a corner kick by Hamm into the net.

Cindy Parlow (*No. 12*) uses her head in the game against Brazil.

Defender Joy Fawcett sealed the U.S. victory with a near-post header. President Clinton and his family were on hand to cheer for the home team.

The Brazil-Nigeria game was one of the most exciting of the tournament, although it didn't start out that way. In the first half Brazil was ahead 3–0, and it looked like Nigeria was going to be blown away. But Nigeria scored three goals in the second half to tie the game! The match went into sudden-death overtime, and Sissi calmly scored the "golden goal" in the 104th minute to give her team the victory—and a berth in the semifinals.

With the quarterfinals over, Russia finished with the worst record and failed to qualify for the Olympics. Only the top seven quarterfinalists were allowed to compete at the Sydney 2000 Games because Australia automatically held the eighth spot in the tournament as the host country.

The Semifinals

July 4:   U. S.   vs.   B R A Z I L

The real fireworks on this Fourth of July were in Palo Alto, California, at the U.S.–Brazil semifinal game in Stanford Stadium. The American men had faced Brazil in the same stadium on the same day in the 1994 World Cup! The men lost 1–0, but the U.S. women weren't about to let history repeat itself.

The United States got over its previous shaky starts and came out strong, scoring in the fifth minute. Foudy sent a ball into the box that Brazilian keeper Maravilha got both hands on but couldn't control. Cindy Parlow headed home the loose ball to put the U.S. ahead 1–0. The Brazilians fought hard and had some good chances to score, but Scurry made several key saves in what she called the best game of her life. At the end of the second half, Hamm drew a foul in the penalty box, and Akers nailed the PK, giving the American women a 2–0 win.

The Semifinals

July 4

China faced Norway at Foxboro Stadium near Boston in the other semifinal match. The game between these two giants of women's soccer was expected to be close, but Norway couldn't stop the phenomenal Chinese attack. By capitalizing on set plays like corner kicks and free kicks, China was up 4–0 by the 65th minute. Sun Wen scored once in the first half and converted a penalty kick at the end of the game to make the final score 5–0. Norway would not be a two-time world champion. The final would be a rematch of the 1996 Olympic gold-medal game between the United States and China.

The Third-place Game

July 10

Before the championship game began, Brazil faced Norway to decide third place. The two teams were well matched: Brazil's ball skills and speed balanced Norway's strength and experience. Both teams had good scoring chances but the game remained scoreless at the end of regulation. The game went directly to penalty kicks, so that the championship game would start on time. Each team made four of its first five PKs. Then Norway's Ann Kristin Aarones sent her penalty kick flying over the goal. Formiga kicked next for Brazil and scored, winning the game and giving the Brazilian women their first top-three finish in a world championship.

The Final

July 10

It was a hot, sunny day at the Rose Bowl in Pasadena, California, and two of the best teams in women's soccer had gathered to decide the world championship. The crowd of 90,185 was the largest ever for a women's sporting event, breaking the record set at the opening game at Giants Stadium 21 days earlier. Brightly painted faces, homemade signs, soccer chants, and American flags filled the stadium.

The defenses of both teams were tested right from the start. United States defenders Kate Sobrero, Brandi Chastain, and Carla Overbeck put up a wall that the Chinese just couldn't break through. The Chinese defense was just as tough on the American team.

WOMEN'S WORLD CUP
FINAL STANDINGS

The First Round

Three points were awarded for a win, one point for a tie, and zero points for a loss.

Group A

TEAM	W	L	T	GF	GA	PTS
U.S.	3	0	0	13	1	9
Nigeria	2	1	0	5	8	6
North Korea	1	2	0	4	6	3
Denmark	0	3	0	1	8	0

U.S. 3, Denmark 0   Nigeria 2, North Korea 1   U.S. 7, Nigeria 1
North Korea 3, Denmark 1   Nigeria 2, Denmark 0   U.S. 3, North Korea 0

Group B

TEAM	W	L	T	GF	GA	PTS
Brazil	2	0	1	12	4	7
Germany	1	0	2	10	4	5
Italy	1	1	1	3	3	4
Mexico	0	3	0	1	15	0

Brazil 7, Mexico 1   Germany 1, Italy 1   Brazil 2, Italy 0
Germany 6, Mexico 0   Germany 3, Brazil 3   Italy 2, Mexico 0

Group C

TEAM	W	L	T	GF	GA	PTS
Norway	3	0	0	13	2	9
Russia	2	1	0	10	3	6
Canada	0	2	1	3	12	1
Japan	0	2	1	1	10	1

Japan 1, Canada 1   Norway 2, Russia 1   Norway 7, Canada 1
Russia 5, Japan 0   Russia 4, Canada 1   Norway 4, Japan 0

Group D

TEAM	W	L	T	GF	GA	PTS
China	3	0	0	12	2	9
Sweden	2	1	0	6	3	6
Australia	0	2	1	3	7	1
Ghana	0	2	1	1	10	1

China 2, Sweden 1   Australia 1, Ghana 1   Sweden 3, Australia 1
China 7, Ghana 0   China 3, Australia 1   Sweden 2, Ghana 0

The Quarterfinals

China 2, Russia 0	Norway 3, Sweden 1
U.S. 3, Germany 2	Brazil 4, Nigeria 3 (OT)

The Semifinals

U.S. 2, Brazil 0	China 5, Norway 0

The Third-place Game

Brazil 0, Norway 0 (Brazil wins 5-4 on penalty kicks)

The Final

U.S. 0, China 0 (U.S. wins 5-4 on penalty kicks)

The game was scoreless as it neared the end of the second half.

Michelle Akers was ferocious on defense and expertly organized the U.S. attack. In the second minute of injury time, Scurry and Akers both leaped to clear a Chinese corner kick. Scurry's punch ended up connecting with Akers's head. Suffering from a slight concussion and heat exhaustion, Akers was escorted to the locker room for medical attention. Sara Whalen subbed in as the first 15-minute period of sudden-death overtime started.

China would have won the game 10 minutes into the first overtime period if not for Kristine Lilly. During a Chinese corner kick, Scurry came off her line to attempt a save. China's Fan Yunjie headed the ball past Scurry, but Lilly was standing guard and headed it away, saving the U.S. team. At the end of the first overtime period, the game was still 0–0.

The game remained scoreless through the second overtime period. The world championship would be decided by penalty kicks. Each team selected five players to take the PKs. The teams would alternate kickers, with China shooting first. The initial two kicks by both teams went in. The third kicker for China, Liu Ying, stepped up. Scurry dived to the left and blocked her shot! If the U.S. players made the rest of their shots, they would win!

11 JULIE FOUDY

| POSITION: | Midfielder | HEIGHT: | 5 feet 6 inches | BORN: | January 23, 1971 |
| GOALS: | 32 | WEIGHT: | 130 pounds | UNIFORM NUMBER: | 11 |

GAMES PLAYED WITH THE NATIONAL TEAM: 166

One of the team captains, Julie is a vocal leader; if you listen carefully during games, you can often hear her voice. In fact, sometimes she is called "Loudy." She has led the midfield through three World Cups and an Olympics.

Julie Maurine Foudy grew up in Mission Viejo, California. She attended Mission Viejo High School and was named Southern California's Player of the Year three years in a row (1987–89). A four-time All-American at Stanford University, she was named *Soccer America*'s Player of the Year in 1991. Julie had 52 goals and 32 assists in her Stanford career. She earned a degree in biology and was accepted into Stanford medical school but decided not to pursue medicine. She married Ian Sawyers in 1995.

Making her national-team debut in 1988, Julie has been a fixture on the team ever since. She is third on America's all-time caps (games played with the national team) list with 166. After playing as a defensive midfielder in the 1995 Women's World Cup and the 1996 Olympics, Julie has switched to a more attacking midfield role. She scored her first hat trick in 1998, and she scored a goal in the American team's first game of the 1999 Women's World Cup. In addition to playing soccer, Julie has also been doing work as an announcer for ESPN.

DID YOU KNOW? Julie Foudy won the 1997 FIFA Fair Play Award for her work to prevent child labor being used in the making of soccer balls in Pakistan.

9 MIA HAMM

POSITION: Forward	HEIGHT: 5 feet 5 inches	BORN: March 17, 1972
GOALS: 114	WEIGHT: 125 pounds	UNIFORM NUMBER: 9

GAMES PLAYED WITH THE NATIONAL TEAM: 183

Al Bello/Allsport

Mia has often been called the greatest female soccer player on earth. When she attacks the goal, her strength and grace are hard to believe. She has scored more goals for her national team than any other person on the planet, past or present. She broke the world scoring record of 107 goals on May 22, 1999.

Mariel Margaret Hamm was born in Selma, Alabama. Growing up in a military family, Mia moved around a lot as a kid. She went to Lake Braddock Secondary School in Burke, Virginia, and Notre Dame High School in Wichita Falls, Texas. By the time she started college at the University of North Carolina (UNC) in 1989, she had already been playing for the national team for two years! Mia led UNC to four NCAA Division I national championships. She also was named the top college player in the country two years in a row (1992–93). She graduated from UNC with a degree in political science and married Christiaan Corry, a Marine Corps pilot, in 1994.

Mia's first appearance with the national team was in August 1987 at the age of 15. Since then she has won two World Cups and an Olympic gold medal. She also leads the team in assists. Opponents often double-team Mia, so she has become an expert at setting up a goal by passing the ball to an open teammate. Another category she leads the U.S. team in is hat tricks—she has scored three goals in a game nine times.

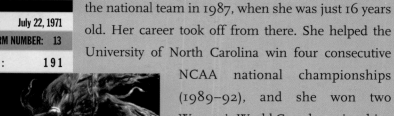

13 KRISTINE LILLY

POSITION: Midfielder	HEIGHT: 5 feet 4 inches	BORN: July 22, 1971
GOALS: 81	WEIGHT: 125 pounds	UNIFORM NUMBER: 13

GAMES PLAYED WITH THE NATIONAL TEAM: 191

Kris has played more times for her national team than any other player in history—male or female. Her experience certainly shows in her mastery of the game. She always seems to be in the right spot at the right time—like when she saved the game by clearing a would-be goal off the line in overtime during the final of the 1999 Women's World Cup.

Raised in Wilton, Connecticut, Kristine Marie Lilly led Wilton High School to three state championships. She played her first game with the national team in 1987, when she was just 16 years old. Her career took off from there. She helped the University of North Carolina win four consecutive NCAA national championships (1989–92), and she won two Women's World Cup championships (1991 and 1999) and an Olympic gold medal (1996).

Besides her amazing talent and fitness, Kris is most known for her great attitude. Her name often comes up when young members of the national team are asked who they admire most. A little-known fact is that she played with the Continental Indoor Soccer League's Washington Warthogs, a men's pro indoor soccer team, in 1995.

16 TIFFENY MILBRETT

POSITION: Forward	HEIGHT: 5 feet 2 inches	BORN: October 23, 1972
GOALS: 68	WEIGHT: 130 pounds	UNIFORM NUMBER: 16

GAMES PLAYED WITH THE NATIONAL TEAM: 129

Tiffeny is the second member of the U.S. team's front line. She scored a career-high 20 goals and added 12 assists in 1999. The team's shortest player, Tiffeny is great at weaving through defenders to score a goal or set up her teammates.

Tiffeny Carleen Milbrett grew up in Portland, Oregon. While attending Hillsboro High School, she set state records with 54 goals in a season and 131 in her high-school career.

In 1990, she started her college career with the University of Portland. She was named *Soccer America*'s Freshman of the Year. Tiffeny is Portland's all-time leading scorer with 103 goals. She was tied for first place with Mia Hamm as the NCAA Division I all-time leading goal scorer until the record was broken by Danielle Fotopoulos in 1998.

Tiffeny debuted with the U.S. National Team in August 1991. She scored three goals at the 1995 Women's World Cup, two goals at the Olympics (including the game winner against China in the gold-medal match), and another three at the 1999 Women's World Cup. She also set a team record with five assists in a match versus Australia on June 5, 1997. From 1995–97, Tiffeny also played for Shiroki Serena in Japan's pro women's league.

4 CARLA OVERBECK

POSITION: Defender	HEIGHT: 5 feet 7 inches	BORN: May 9, 1968
GOALS: 7	WEIGHT: 125 pounds	UNIFORM NUMBER: 4

GAMES PLAYED WITH THE NATIONAL TEAM: 155

The team's co-captain, Carla has been anchoring the defense for more than 10 years. Her experience and confidence make her a natural leader. She's called the "Iron Woman" of the team, and there's a good reason for it: she started every game of the 1991, 1995, and 1999 Women's World Cups, and the 1996 Olympics! In fact, she once played in 63 consecutive games, which is a U.S. Women's National Team record.

Carla Werden grew up in Dallas, Texas, where she played volleyball, basketball, and soccer at Richardson

High School. She went on to play soccer for the University of North Carolina and won the national championship each year she was there. She graduated from UNC in 1990 with a degree in psychology.

All of Carla's accomplishments on the field are even more amazing when you consider that she found time to become a mother. She married Greg Overbeck in 1992, and after the Olympics she took a year off from the team to have a baby. She became a true "soccer mom" when her son Jackson was born on August 14, 1997. Just two months later, Carla was back on the field with the national team! During training camp for the 1999 Women's World Cup, the team had a nanny to help care for Carla's son and Joy Fawcett's two daughters.

12 CINDY PARLOW

POSITION: Forward	HEIGHT: 5 feet 11 inches	BORN: May 8, 1978
GOALS: 26	WEIGHT: 145 pounds	UNIFORM NUMBER: 12

GAMES PLAYED WITH THE NATIONAL TEAM: 67

Cindy, "CP" for short, was named the top player in college soccer in 1997 and 1998. She is an excellent header and is very good in the penalty area.

Parlow's height nicely complements smaller forwards like Hamm and Milbrett.

Cynthia Marie Parlow grew up in Memphis, Tennessee, where she was named the 1994 Tennessee High School Player of the Year at Germantown High. The all-time state leader in assists, she had 83 in her high-school career. CP went to the University of North Carolina after graduating from high school in just three years. She helped lead UNC to two NCAA Division I championships (1996–97). Cindy finished her career with the Tar Heels with 68 goals and 53 assists.

Since her debut with the national team in January 1996, Cindy has become one of the top-10 goal scorers in U.S. Women's National Team history with 26 goals. The 21-year-old was the youngest member of the gold-medal-winning 1996 Olympic Team, and she scored two goals at the 1999 Women's World Cup.

1 BRIANA SCURRY

POSITION: Goalkeeper	HEIGHT: 5 feet 8 inches	BORN: September 7, 1971
GOALS AGAINST AVERAGE: 0.61	WEIGHT: 150 pounds	UNIFORM NUMBER: 1
GAMES PLAYED WITH THE NATIONAL TEAM:		98

Briana, "Bri" for short, has been the top goalkeeper for the United States for the last five years. She played every minute of every game in the last Olympics, as well as in the 1999 World Cup. In fact, the U.S. has only lost eight times with Bri in net. She is known for her amazing agility and her high vertical leap.

Briana Collette Scurry grew up in Dayton, Minnesota. A star athlete in high school, she led Anoka Senior High to the state championship in 1989. Her success continued at the University of Massachusetts (UMass), where she had 37 shutouts in 65 starts. During her senior year in 1993, Bri led UMass to the semifinals of the NCAA championship and won two national goalkeeper of the year awards. She graduated with a degree in political science.

Bri first appeared with the national team in March 1994. She is now the Americans' most capped goalkeeper, having played for her country 98 times. One of her finest goalkeeping moments came in the championship game of the 1999 Women's World Cup. The final came down to penalty kicks. The third Chinese kicker was Liu Ying. Bri dived to her left and blocked Liu's kick, setting up the American victory. The image of her celebrating the save with her fist raised in the air is one soccer fans won't soon forget.

20 KATE SOBRERO

POSITION: Defender	HEIGHT: 5 feet 7 inches	BORN: August 23, 1976
GOALS: 0	WEIGHT: 135 pounds	UNIFORM NUMBER: 20
GAMES PLAYED WITH THE NATIONAL TEAM:		34

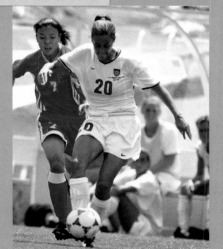

Kate has become a key center defender on the U.S. team. She made her national-team debut in April 1998, and by the time the 1999 Women's World Cup came around, she was a starting defender, winning the position over more experienced players.

Kathryn Michele Sobrero grew up in Bloomfield Hills, Michigan. As a freshman in high school, she led Detroit Country Day to the 1991 state championship. Moving on to Notre Dame University, she started every game the Fighting Irish played during her four years there. Notre Dame won the 1995 NCAA Division I championship, and she was named the Defensive MVP of the tournament. Kate graduated from Notre Dame with a degree in science-business.

Kate helped the U.S. Under-20 National Team win the Nordic Cup championship in 1997 before joining the full national team. She actually first trained with the national team in 1995, but she had some bad luck—she fainted during fitness testing! The second time she was invited to training camp, in January 1998, she broke her jaw in a collision with goalkeeper Tracy Ducar! She finally got her start with the national team in April 1998, and now she has a Women's World Cup championship to show for it.

5 | TIFFANY ROBERTS

POSITION: Midfielder	HEIGHT: 5 feet 4 inches	BORN: May 5, 1977
GOALS: 6	WEIGHT: 112 pounds	UNIFORM NUMBER: 5

GAMES PLAYED WITH THE NATIONAL TEAM: 79

Tiffany is sometimes called the "Energizer Bunny" because she has so much energy on the field. She made her debut with the national team when she was only 16. She was a member of the 1995 Women's World Cup and 1996 Olympic teams. She finished her career at the University of North Carolina in 1998 with her best season ever, scoring three goals and adding 12 assists in 26 games. Tiffany is usually not a starter, but she often plays an important role coming off the bench. She grew up in San Ramon, California, and was also a top track athlete in high school.

2 | LORRIE FAIR

POSITION: Defender	HEIGHT: 5 feet 3 inches	BORN: August 5, 1978
GOALS: 1	WEIGHT: 125 pounds	UNIFORM NUMBER: 2

GAMES PLAYED WITH THE NATIONAL TEAM: 51

This 21-year-old has been with the national team since her freshman year at the University of North Carolina. She didn't make the 1996 Olympic team, but she was the youngest member of the 1999 Women's World Cup Team, seeing action in four games. She just finished her last year at UNC and helped the Tar Heels win three NCAA titles. Lorrie was a member of the U.S. Under-20 National Team from 1994 to 1998. Her full name is Lorraine Ming Fair, and she has a twin sister named Ronnie, who has also played for the national team.

THE SUBSTITUTES

22 | DANIELLE FOTOPOULOS

POSITION: Forward	HEIGHT: 5 feet 11 inches	BORN: March 24, 1976
GOALS: 11	WEIGHT: 165 pounds	UNIFORM NUMBER: 22

GAMES PLAYED WITH THE NATIONAL TEAM: 26

Danielle led the University of Florida (UF) to its first NCAA championship in 1998, scoring the winning goal to upset UNC 1–0. She finished her college career with an amazing 118 goals, breaking the NCAA career goal-scoring record previously held by Mia Hamm and Tiffeny Milbrett. The 5-foot-11-inch forward seems to be able to put the ball in the goal from just about anywhere. Formerly Danielle Garrett, she married George Fotopoulos in 1996. She grew up in Altamonte Springs, Florida. Danielle graduated from UF with a degree in leisure management.

8 | SHANNON MACMILLAN

POSITION: Forward	HEIGHT: 5 feet 5 inches	BORN: October 7, 1974
GOALS: 22	WEIGHT: 130 pounds	UNIFORM NUMBER: 8

GAMES PLAYED WITH THE NATIONAL TEAM: 89

Shannon is often called a "super sub" because she can come off the bench and score or assist on game-winning goals. She proved her effectiveness at the 1996 Olympics, when she scored the overtime "golden goal" versus Norway in the semifinals. She saw playing time in each game of the 1999 World Cup, contributing one goal and three assists. A graduate of the University of Portland, Shannon was named the top college player of the year in 1995. She grew up in Escondido, California.

3 CHRISTIE PEARCE

POSITION: Defender	HEIGHT: 5 feet 6 inches	BORN: June 24, 1975
GOALS: 2	WEIGHT: 140 pounds	UNIFORM NUMBER: 3

GAMES PLAYED WITH THE NATIONAL TEAM: 55

Christie first appeared with the national team in 1997. She has become a solid defensive player, sharing time with Lorrie Fair on the back line. Christie grew up in Point Pleasant, New Jersey, and is a graduate of Monmouth University (New Jersey), where she holds the all-time scoring record in soccer and also excelled as a basketball player. She graduated with a degree in special education and is working toward her teaching certificate.

24 TRACY DUCAR

POSITION: Goalkeeper	HEIGHT: 5 feet 7 inches	BORN: June 18, 1973
GOALS AGAINST AVERAGE: 0.57	WEIGHT: 140 pounds	UNIFORM NUMBER: 24

GAMES PLAYED WITH THE NATIONAL TEAM: 24

Tracy has been challenging Scurry for the No.1 goalkeeper position for several years. She grew up in North Andover, Massachusetts, and led the University of North Carolina to the NCAA championship in 1994. Tracy is better than Scurry at coming out of the box and has strong field skills, but she hasn't pulled off the amazing saves that Scurry has. Her maiden name is Noonan, and she married Chris Ducar in 1997. She holds a degree in biology with a minor in chemistry.

15 TISHA VENTURINI

POSITION: Midfielder	HEIGHT: 5 feet 6 inches	BORN: March 3, 1973
GOALS: 43	WEIGHT: 125 pounds	UNIFORM NUMBER: 15

GAMES PLAYED WITH THE NATIONAL TEAM: 128

Tisha was named the top college player in the country in 1994, during her senior year at the University of North Carolina. A regular starter with the national team from 1993 to 1997, she has been playing more of a substitute role since the team started using only three midfielders. Tisha is one of the highest-scoring midfielders in U.S. history and has a knack for getting important goals. Tisha, whose middle name is Lea, grew up in Modesto, California.

18 SASKIA WEBBER

POSITION: Goalkeeper	HEIGHT: 5 feet 9 inches	BORN: June 13, 1971
GOALS AGAINST AVERAGE: 0.64	WEIGHT: 145 pounds	UNIFORM NUMBER: 18

GAMES PLAYED WITH THE NATIONAL TEAM: 27

Saskia made a comeback in 1998 and earned a spot on the 1999 World Cup Team. Previous to 1998, she hadn't played for the national team since 1995. She debuted for the national team back in 1992 and was a member of the 1995 World Cup team, playing in one game against Australia. She went to Rutgers University and still holds the school record for career shutouts. Her full name is Saskia Johanna Webber, and she grew up in Princeton, New Jersey.

7 SARA WHALEN

POSITION: Defender	HEIGHT: 5 feet 6 inches	BORN: April 28, 1976
GOALS: 3	WEIGHT: 130 pounds	UNIFORM NUMBER: 7

GAMES PLAYED WITH THE NATIONAL TEAM: 42

Sara is a multitalented player who usually plays defense but was also a very successful striker during her senior year at the University of Connecticut. One of the fastest players on the national team, she has been a key substitute since she made her debut in April 1997. When the team needed someone to take the place of Michelle Akers at the end of the 1999 World Cup final, Sara stepped in. Sara, whose middle name is Eve, grew up in Greenlawn, New York.

6

THE ROAD TO
SYDNEY

The 2000 Olympics AUSTRALIA

The second women's Olympic soccer tournament will take place in September 2000. The best teams in the world will gather in the Australian cities of Sydney, Melbourne, and Canberra—each hoping to be the one that takes home the gold.

Becoming one of the eight Olympic teams was not an easy accomplishment. Sixty-three teams from around the world, from Swaziland to Samoa, took part in the 1999 Women's World Cup qualifying contests. Only 16 made the final cut and won the right to play at the 1999 Women's World Cup in the United States. Out of those 16, only eight qualified for the Olympics in Sydney.

Prior to the tournament, FIFA announced that the teams who finished in the top eight at the Women's World Cup would qualify for the Olympics. There

was one catch, though. The Australians were automatically in since the Olympics were being held in their country. If they didn't make it into the top eight, then only the top seven teams would qualify.

Australia had a tough World Cup and was knocked out in the first round, meaning that only seven of the eight quarterfinalists would go to the Olympics.

The four teams that won in the quarterfinals (Brazil, China, Norway, and the United States) automatically qualified. Out of the four teams that lost (Germany, Nigeria, Russia, and Sweden), the one that lost by the most points would not make it. It came down to Sweden and Russia. Sweden lost to Norway 3–1, and Russia lost to China 2–0. They both lost by two goals, but Sweden qualified

ROSELI

POSITION: Forward   BORN: September 7, 1969

Roseli is one of the world's best forwards, but she didn't get to play in the 1999 Women's World Cup because of a leg injury. She has fully recovered and seems to have regained her magical dribbling skills. Before her injury in 1999, she had the amazing record of 31 goals in 24 games! Brazil has steadily improved, placing fifth in the 1996 Olympics and then third in the 1999 Women's World Cup. Roseli will be looking to lead her team to an even better finish in 2000. Her full name is Roseli de Belo, and she plays for the Brazilian club São Paulo.

BRAZIL

BENTE NORDBY

POSITION: Goalkeeper   BORN: July 23, 1974

Nordby is one of the world's top goalkeepers. She has been with the Norwegian national team a long time—through three World Cups and an Olympic tournament. Nordby is a key reason why Norway is the only country with a winning record against the United States. At six and a half feet tall, Nordby is an imposing figure and can reach almost any corner of the goal. With her experience and talent, opponents should have an extremely difficult time scoring on Norway in the 2000 Olympics.

NORWAY

SISSI

POSITION: Midfielder   **BORN: June 2, 1967**

An amazing midfielder, Sissi (pronounced see-see) led Brazil to third place at the 1999 Women's World Cup—her national team's best finish ever. She played every minute of every game, and she was awarded the Golden Shoe for being the top scorer of the tournament. She is fast, is accurate with her shots, and has great one-on-one moves. Sissi also played in the 1996 Olympics. Sydney 2000 may be the 32-year-old's last chance to shoot for Olympic gold. Sissi's full name is Sisleide Lima do Amor, and she plays with Roseli on the Brazilian club São Paulo.

BRAZIL

JANE TORNQVIST

POSITION: Defender   **BORN: May 9, 1975**

This tough defender has been with the Swedish national team since she was 20 years old. Tornqvist has a rare knack for scoring goals from her defensive position. In fact, she notched one in Sweden's second game of the 1999 Women's World Cup against Australia. The young Swedish team barely squeezed by Russia to qualify for the 2000 Olympics. It will be relying on a strong defense to get them to the medal rounds in Sydney.

SWEDEN

WANG LIPING

POSITION: Defender BORN: November 12, 1973

Wang was one of the most outstanding defenders of the 1999 Women's World Cup. Her tackling and marking skills are just about perfect. She played every minute of every game in the 1999 Women's World Cup, and with her help the Chinese team only gave up two goals the whole tournament. With over 70 caps with the Chinese team, Wang has plenty of experience defending against some of the world's best forwards. Wang plays for the club team Hebei in China's Elite League.

CHINA

Tom Hauck/Allsport

BETTINA WIEGMANN

POSITION: Midfielder   BORN: October 7, 1971

Wiegmann really shined at the 1999 World Cup, distinguishing herself as one of the tournament's best midfielders. She scored three goals and was tough on defense, but Germany finished a disappointing sixth. Wiegmann also played a key role in her team's semifinal game at the 1995 Women's World Cup—it was her goal that allowed Germany to beat China 1–0 and advance to the championship game. However, Germany lost to Norway in the final, and it has never won a major world championship. Wiegmann will be out to change that at the 2000 Olympics.

JBW/International Sports Images

GERMANY

All-American: a player who has been selected by the National Soccer Coaches Association of America (NSCAA) as one of the best in the nation in the past high-school or college season.

caps: games played with a national team.

clear: to kick or head the ball long and high, sometimes out of bounds, to prevent the attacking team from scoring.

defender: a player who is in the back of her team's formation, closest to her own goal. Her main job is to get the ball away from opponents and prevent them from scoring. Also called a back or fullback.

direct free kick: a kick awarded to the opposing team of a player who has committed one of the 10 fouls punishable by a direct free kick. A goal can be scored on a direct free kick.

draw: a game that ends with the score tied.

far post: the goal post farthest from the ball.

FIFA (Federation Internationale de Football Association): the world governing body of soccer in charge of organizing major international tournaments like the Women's World Cup. (Pronounced fee-fa.)

flank: the area of the field near the sidelines, often used to describe defenders, midfielders, or forwards who play in that area.

forward: a player who is in the front of her team's formation, closest to her opponent's goal. Her main job is to attack the other team's goal and score.

foul: the breaking of one of the rules of soccer. Also called an offense or infraction.

goalkeeper: the player who guards the goal. The goalkeeper is the only player who is allowed to touch the ball with her hands.

goal kick: a kick to restart play, usually taken by a defender or goalkeeper on the defending team, after the ball has been knocked over the goal line by the attacking team.

goal line: the line that the goal sits on. It defines the edge of the playing field and runs from corner flag to corner flag.

goals against (GA): the total number of goals that have been scored against a team.

goals against average (GAA): the average number of goals a goalkeeper allows in a game.

goals for (GF): the total number of goals that a team has scored.

golden goal: a goal scored in sudden-death overtime that wins a game.

hand ball: a foul called when a player, in the opinion of the referee, has touched the ball on purpose with her hand or arm.

hat trick: three goals scored in a game by one player.

header: when a player hits the ball with her head, usually in an attempt to score.

Hermann Trophy: an award given to the best male and best female college player of the year.

indirect free kick: a kick awarded to the opposing team of a player who has committed one of the eight fouls punishable by an indirect free kick. The ball must be touched by another player before a goal can be scored.

injury time: time (usually one to four minutes) added to the end of each half of a game by a referee to make up for time lost when the game was paused for injuries, substitutions, etc. Also called extra time or stoppage time.

instep: the front of the foot, usually where a shoe's laces are.

MAC Award: the Missouri Athletic Club Award, given to the best male and best female college player of the year.

man down: when a team is playing with only 10 players because one of its players received a red card and was sent off the field.

midfielder: a player who is in the middle of her team's formation. Her job is to help attack and defend.

national team: a team that represents a country in international competition, made up of that country's best players.

near post: the goal post closest to the ball.

NSCAA (National Soccer Coaches Association of America): the national organization of soccer coaches in the United States.

ODP (Olympic Development Program): a program run by the United States Soccer Federation (USSF) that attempts to identify and train high-level youth players in order to produce future national-team players.

offside: when a player is closer to her opponent's goal than the ball and has less than two opponents in front of her. Being offside is only an offense if the player is interfering with the play or gaining some advantage by being in that position.

one-touch: when a player receives a ball and passes or shoots it with her first touch, without trapping or dribbling it.

overtime: an additional period of time played at the end of a game that is used to break a tie.

own goal: a goal scored after last being touched by a member of the defending team. It counts as a goal for the attacking team.

penalty area: the area in front of the goal that is 44 yards wide and 18 yards long. Inside this area, direct free kicks awarded to the attacking team become penalty kicks.

penalty kick: a kick awarded to the attacking team after the defending team has committed a foul inside the penalty area that is punishable by a direct free kick. The kick is taken from the penalty spot 12 yards from the goal.

penalty kick shoot-out: a series of penalty kicks used to determine the winner after regulation and overtime periods of a game have ended in a tie. Five kicks are taken by each team, and the team that scores more goals wins. If the teams are still tied, the kicks continue until one team has scored more goals than the other after the same number of kicks.

qualifying: the games a team plays in order to win the right to play in a tournament.

red card: a card shown to a player by a referee when she is ejected for committing a very serious foul. The player must leave the field and cannot be replaced. Her team must play the rest of the game with one less player.

save: when a goalkeeper prevents a goal from being scored by catching or deflecting the ball.

striker: a forward whose main job is to score goals.

sweeper: a defender who plays behind the other defenders and "sweeps up" any attackers that get through the line of defense.

tackle: to take the ball away from an opponent. To be a fair tackle, the tackler must contact the ball first, not the player.

TFC (The Football Confederation): the world is divided into six soccer regions. TFC includes the countries in North America, Central America, and the Caribbean. Each region holds qualifying tournaments to determine which countries play in FIFA tournaments like the World Cup. TFC was formerly called the Confederation of North, Central America, and Caribbean Association Football (CONCACAF).

throw-in: the method of putting the ball back into play after it has gone over a touchline. The opposing team of the player who last touched the ball gets the throw-in.

touchline: the sideline.

trap: to bring the ball under control, usually with the foot, thigh, or chest.

USSF (United States Soccer Federation): the governing body of soccer in the United States. It runs the women's and men's national teams.

volley: to kick the ball while it's in the air.

wing: an outside defender, midfielder, or forward who is supposed to stay near the sidelines.

yellow card: a card shown to a player when she is cautioned by a referee for committing a serious foul. If a player receives a second yellow card she gets a red card and is sent off the field.

RESOURCES

MAGAZINES

SOCCER JR.
27 Unquowa Road
Fairfield, CT 06430
800-829-5382
www.soccerjr.com

KICK!
30400 Van Dyke Avenue
Warren, MI 48093
773-281-0847
www.kickmag.com

NETWORK
Women's
Soccer Foundation
608 N.E. 63rd Street
Seattle, WA 98115
www.womensoccer.org

SOCCER AMERICA
P.O. Box 23704
Oakland, CA 94623
800-997-6223
www.socceramerica.com

WOMEN'S SOCCER WORLD
1728 Mulberry Street
Montgomery, AL 36106
334-263-0080
www.womensoccer.com

ORGANIZATIONS

AMERICAN YOUTH SOCCER ORGANIZATION (AYSO)
12501 South Isis Avenue
Hawthorne, CA 90250
800-USA-AYSO
(800-872-2976)
www.soccer.org

CANADIAN SOCCER ASSOCIATION
Place Soccer Canada
237 Metcalfe St.
Ottawa, Ontario K2P 1R2
Canada
613-237-7678
www.canoe.ca/
SoccerCanada/home.html

FIFA
P.O. Box 85
8030 Zurich, Switzerland
41-1/384-9595
www.fifa.com

MAJOR LEAGUE SOCCER
110 East 42nd Street
10th Floor
New York, NY 10017
212-450-1200
www.mlsnet.com

1999 WOMEN'S WORLD CUP
Suite 950
1875 Century Park East
Los Angeles, CA 90067
310-286-2992
wwc99.fifa.com

SOCCER ASSOCIATION FOR YOUTH (SAY)
4050 Executive Park Drive
Suite 100
Cincinnati, OH 45241
800-233-7291
www.saysoccer.org

SYDNEY ORGANIZING COMMITTEE FOR THE OLYMPIC GAMES
235 Jones Street
Ultimo Sydney 2007
Australia
61-2/9297-2000
www.olympics.com

U.S. SOCCER FEDERATION
1801 S. Prairie Avenue
Chicago, IL 60616
312-808-1300
www.us-soccer.com

U.S. YOUTH SOCCER ASSOCIATION (USYSA)
899 Presidential Drive
Suite 117
Richardson, TX 75081
800-4-SOCCER
(800-476-2237)
www.youthsoccer.org

WOMEN'S SOCCER FOUNDATION
P.O. Box 600404
Newton, MA 02460
617-243-9487
www.womensoccer.org

CATALOGS

EUROSPORT
431 US Highway 70A East
Hillsborough, NC 27278
Orders: 800-934-3876
Customer Service:
800-487-7253
www.soccer.com

REEDSWAIN
612 Pughtown Road
Spring City, PA 19475
Orders: 800-331-5191
www.reedswain.com

SOCCER LEARNING SYSTEMS
P.O. Box 277
San Ramon, CA 94583
Orders: 800-762-2376
www.soccervideos.com

TSI
4324 S. Alston Avenue
Durham, NC 27713
Orders: 800-842-6679
Customer Service:
800-884-6264
www.tsisoccer.com

Caparaz, Dean. "Sweden 1995 Diary." *Soccer America,* July 3, 1995.

Caparaz, Dean. "Sweden 1995 Diary." *Soccer America,* June 26, 1995.

Caparaz, Dean. "U.S. Falls from Throne." *Soccer America,* July 3, 1995.

Ladda, Shawn. "Ornamental and Useless?" *Soccer Journal,* May/June 1999.

Shots On Goal, vol. 3, no. 5 (1991).

U.S. Soccer Communications Department. *U.S. Soccer 1999 Media Guide.* Chicago, 1999.

Women's World Cup 1999 Organizing Committee, Inc. *1999 FIFA Women's World Cup Media Guide, Tournament Edition.* Los Angeles, 1999.

BIBLIOGRAPHY

INDEX